A Trip to the
FIRE STATION
with SESAME STREET

Christy Peterson

Lerner Publications ◆ Minneapolis

Elmo and his friends from *Sesame Street* are going on a field trip, and you're invited! Field trips provide children with the opportunity to explore their communities, visit new places, and experience hands-on learning. This series brings the joys of field trips to your fingertips. Where will you go next?

—Sincerely, the Editors at Sesame Street

TABLE OF CONTENTS

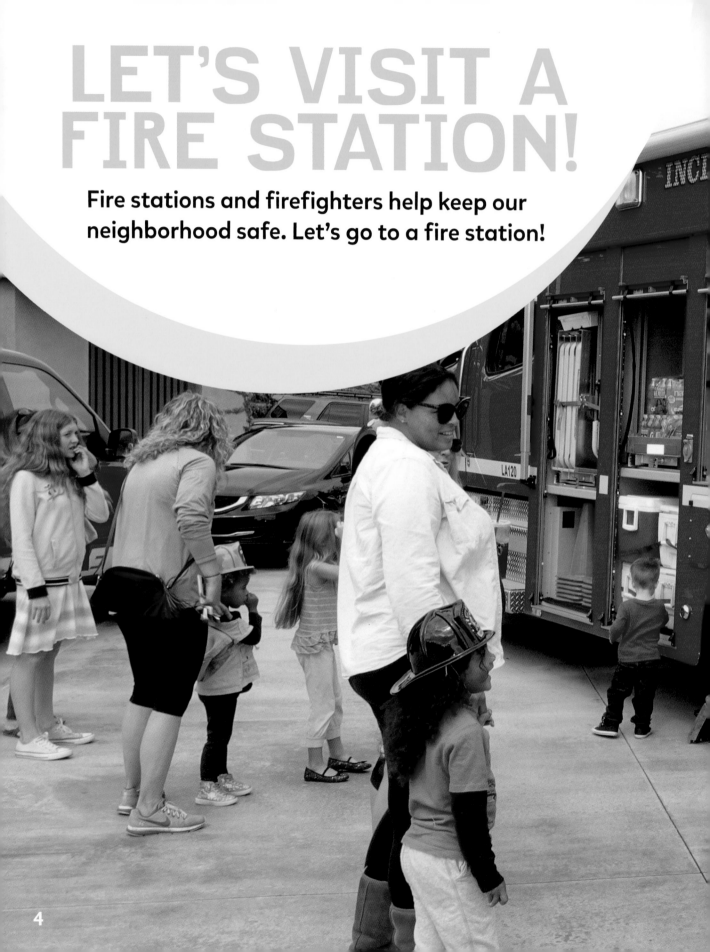

LET'S VISIT A FIRE STATION!

Fire stations and firefighters help keep our neighborhood safe. Let's go to a fire station!

5

We go to the garage first. Look at the fire truck! Firefighters ride inside on their way to fight a fire and help people.

The fire truck has lots of tools.

I see hoses and oxygen tanks.

A ladder truck has
an extra-long ladder.
Firefighters use the ladder
to put out fires in tall
buildings.

9

A pumper truck holds a lot of water to help firefighters put out a fire.

The firefighters show us how they work together to hold the hose.

11

Firefighters wear uniforms to stay safe. Helmets protect their heads. Masks help them breathe clean air. They wear thick clothes and heavy boots and gloves.

Firefighters wear special clothes to keep them safe so they can help keep us safe.

There are always firefighters at the fire station. They take turns cooking in the fire station's kitchen. Sometimes they sleep at the fire station too.

Me ask to make cookies with the firefighters.

An alarm bell goes off to tell the firefighters it's time to go. They put on their uniforms and drive to the fire in their fire trucks.

Firefighters teach us lots of things. They tell us about their trucks and the smoke detectors in our homes.

Smoke detectors beep to let you know there might be a fire.

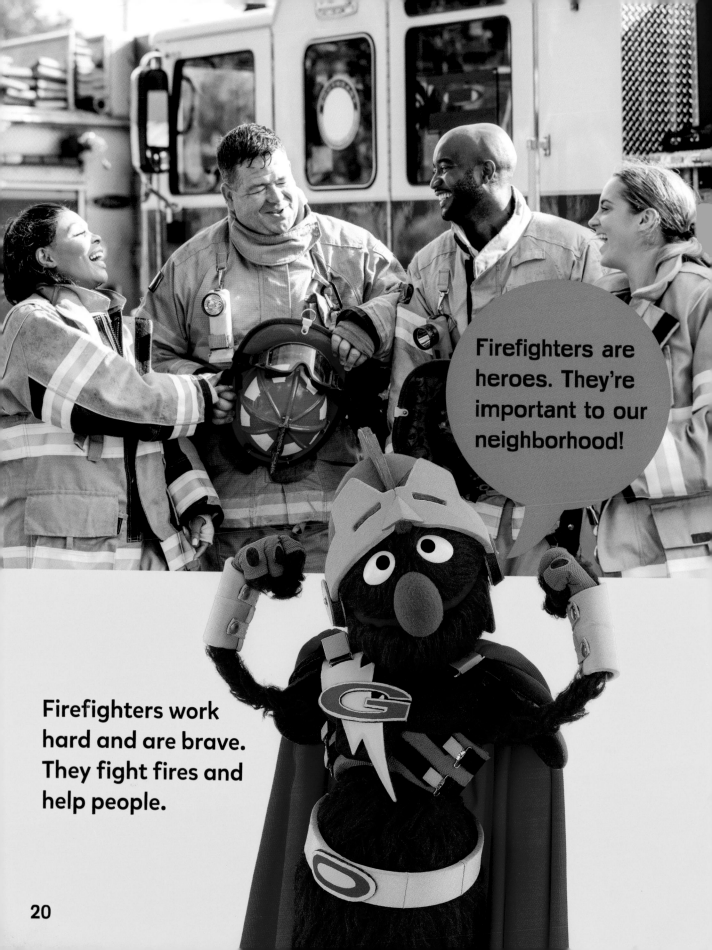

Firefighters are heroes. They're important to our neighborhood!

Firefighters work hard and are brave. They fight fires and help people.

THE FIRE STATION AT HOME

Make a plan with your family to stay safe if a fire happens. Talk to the adults in your home about how to get out safely. Plan a place to meet outside. Practice your plan so everyone knows what to do.

GLOSSARY

alarm: a sound that lets someone know that something is happening

hose: a bendable tube that water can flow through

smoke detector: something that makes a loud noise when there is smoke

uniform: special clothing worn by a group, sometimes so they can do a specific job

LEARN MORE

Bellisario, Gina. *Firefighters in My Community.* Minneapolis: Lerner Publications, 2019.

Boothroyd, Jennifer. *All about Firefighters.* Minneapolis: Lerner Publications, 2021.

McCarthy, Meghan. *Firefighters' Handbook.* New York: Simon & Schuster Books for Young Readers, 2019.

INDEX

PHOTO ACKNOWLEDGMENTS

Image credits: Simone Hogan/Shutterstock.com, pp. 4–5; astudio/Shutterstock.com, p. 6; Robert Hoetink/Shutterstock.com, p. 7 (top); Mint Images/Getty Images, p. 7 (bottom); Nightman1965/Shutterstock.com, p. 8; Donald R. Swartz/Shutterstock.com, p. 10; photo-denver/Shutterstock.com, p. 11; PrasongTakham/Shutterstock.com, p. 12 (top); dcwcreations/Shutterstock.com, p. 12 (bottom); kali9/E+/Getty Images, pp. 13, 20; Helen H. Richardson/The Denver Post via/Getty Images, p. 14; Dusan Petkovic/Shutterstock.com, pp. 16–17; DnHolm/iStock Editorial/Getty Images; Paradise On Earth/Shutterstock.com, p. 19.
Cover: CactuSoup/Getty Images; Mike Powell/The Image Bank RF/Getty Images.

Lerner Publications Company
An imprint of Lerner Publishing Group, Inc.
241 First Avenue North
Minneapolis, MN 55401 USA

For reading levels and more information, look up this title at www.lernerbooks.com.

Main body text set in Mikado a.
Typeface provided by HVD Fonts.

Editor: Rebecca Higgins

Library of Congress Cataloging-in-Publication Data

Names: Peterson, Christy, author.
Title: A trip to the fire station with Sesame Street / Christy Peterson.
Description: Minneapolis : Lerner Publications, [2022] | Series: Sesame Stree field trips | Includes bibliographical references and index. | Audience: Ages 4–8 | Audience: Grades K–1 | Summary: "Kids can tag along to the fire station with firefighter Elmo and other Sesame Street friends! They'll learn about firefighters' gear, fire trucks, and how to make a fire safety plan with their families"—Provided by publisher.
Identifiers: LCCN 2021010508 (print) | LCCN 2021010509 (ebook) | ISBN 9781728439129 (library binding) | ISBN 9781728445069 (ebook)
Subjects: LCSH: Fire departments—Juvenile literature. | Fire fighters—Juvenile literature.
Classification: LCC TH9148 .P454 2022 (print) | LCC TH9148 (ebook) | DDC 363.37—dc23

LC record available at https://lccn.loc.gov/2021010508
LC ebook record available at https://lccn.loc.gov /2021010509

Manufactured in the United States of America
1-49818-49686-9/1/2021